Islam Starter Kit

Islam Starter Kit

Abdalhaqq and Aisha Bewley

DIWAN PRESS

Classical and Contemporary Books on Islam and Sufism

FOUNDED IN 1973

Copyright © Diwan Press Ltd., 2018 CE/1440 AH

Islam Starter Kit

Published by: Diwan Press Ltd.
                      311 Allerton Road
                      Bradford
                      BD15 7HA
                      UK
Website: www.diwanpress.com
E-mail: info@diwanpress.com

This publication is made freely available for the use of
whomever it may prove useful to provided that it is not
exploited for commercial advantage.

Author: Abdalhaqq and Aisha Bewley

Typeset and cover by: Abdassamad Clarke

A catalogue record of this book is available from the
British Library.

ISBN-13:   978-1-908892-66-9 (paperback)

Printed and bound by: Lightning Source

CONTENTS

ISLAM

Islam means Submission, Safety and Peace.

It is the final and complete teaching for all people brought to us by our Master Muhammad, the last of the Messengers of Allah and the Seal of all the Prophets, may Allah bless him and grant him peace. It is supported by five pillars, obligatory for all Muslims.

They are:

1. Shahada   The Witnessing
2. Salat   The Prayer
3. Zakat   The Poor Tax
4. Siyam   The Fast Of Ramadan
5. Hajj   The Pilgrimage To Makka

1. SHAHADA –
THE WITNESSING

This consists of saying:

Ash-hadu an la ilaha illa'llah
I witness that there is no god but Allah
wa ash-hadu anna Muhammada rasulu'llah
And I witness that Muhammad is the
Messenger of Allah.

It is the recognition that there is One God with
no partner who alone is worthy of worship and
that Muhammad, may Allah bless him and
grant him peace, was sent by Allah as the last
of His Messengers with a universal guidance
for all mankind to follow. By making this
affirmation you become a Muslim.

2. SALAT – THE PRAYER

The Prophet Muhammad, may Allah bless him and grant him peace, was commanded to tell his community to pray five times every day. He was shown how to perform the prayer by the Angel Gabriel, and Muslims do the prayer exactly as he was shown it. The first step is purification.

Wudu' – Ablution

Before doing the prayer, all Muslims must purify themselves as follows:

1. Intention: Make the intention to do wudu' and say, *Bismillah* (In the name of Allah)
2. Hands: Wash both hands to the wrists 3 times.
3. Mouth: Rinse out 3 times.
4. Nose: Snuff up water and blow out 3 times.
5. Face: Rub with water thoroughly using both hands 3 times.

6. Forearms: Rub vigorously with water up to and including the elbows, first right and then left, making sure that water goes between the fingers. Do each arm 3 times.
7. Head: Pass the hands over the head from the forehead to the nape of the neck and bring them back to the forehead once.

8. Ears:	Wet both thumbs and forefingers and rub inside and out, once.
9. Feet:	Rub with water all over, including the ankles, first right then left. Do each foot 3 times.
10. Shahada:	Raise the forefinger of the right hand and say:

ash-hadu an la ilaha illa'llah

I witness that there is no god but Allah

wa ash-hadu anna Muhammada rasulu'llah

And I witness that Muhammad
is the Messenger of Allah.

Causes which break Wudu'

The things which break wudu' are:
1. Urinating
2. defecating
3. passing wind
4. deep sleep
5. touching the sexual organs
6. sexual contact
7. loss of consciousness

If you are in doubt about your wudu' you do it again.

You must be in wudu' to say the prayer or touch an Arabic copy of the Qur'an.

Always take water with the right hand.

Do not be extravagant with it even if there is a lot.

Be quick but thorough.

After urinating or defecating, the private parts should be thoroughly cleansed with water from any traces of urine and faeces in order for your wudu' to be valid.

Tayammum – Purification with Earth

If there is no water, or using water would be harmful to your health, you do tayammum.

1. Make a specific intention to purify yourself by doing tayammum for the prayer you are about to perform. Say: **Bismillah**.
2. Pat the bare earth firmly with both hands.
3. Blow off any excess dust.
4. Wipe your face thoroughly with both hands.
5. Pat the earth again.
6. Wipe the hands and forearms to the elbows once, first right then left.
7. Raise the forefinger of the right hand and say the shahada.

Tayammum may also be done using a flat stone instead of dry earth.

Tayammum is the same as wudu' except that tayammum must be done immediately before each obligatory prayer.

Ghusl-Bathing

Certain things necessitate the washing of the whole body. They are:

1. male seminal discharge
2. sexual intercourse
3. the end of menstruation
4. the end of lochia bleeding after childbirth

First, you make the intention to purify the whole body and say: *Bismillah.*

Then wash the private parts.

Then do wudu'.

Then wash your head and neck three times, making sure that water penetrates to the roots of the hair and beard.

Then wash the right side of the body, then the left, then the right leg, then the left.

Every part of the body must be rubbed with water.

After you finish, raise the forefinger of the right hand and say the Shahada.

If a ghusl is required, you must do it before the next obligatory prayer.

If that is impossible, then purify yourself with tayammum for the prayer until you are able to do ghusl.

Other times that it is recommended to do ghusl are on becoming a Muslim and before the Jumu'a prayer.

Adhan – the Call to Prayer

This is only obligatory in the mosque. Otherwise it is optional. It must be recited in Arabic.

1. *Allahu Akbar, Allahu Akbar*
   Allah is greater, Allah is greater
2. *ash-hadu an la ilaha illa'llah, ash-hadu an la ilaha illa'llah*
   I witness that there is no god but Allah, I witness that there is no god but Allah
3. *ash-hadu anna Muhammada'r-rasulullah, ash-hadu anna Muhammada'r-rasulullah*
   I witness that Muhammad is the Messenger of Allah, I witness that Muhammad is the Messenger of Allah

4. *hayya 'ala's-salah, hayya 'ala's-salah*
   Come to the prayer, come to the prayer
5. *hayya 'ala'l-falah, hayya 'ala'l-falah*
   Come to success, come to success
6. *Allahu Akbar, Allahu Akbar*
   Allah is greater, Allah is greater
7. *la ilaha illa'llah*
   There is no god but Allah

Iqama – The Call at the Start of Prayer

This must be recited out loud before each obligatory prayer, in Arabic.

1. *Allahu Akbar, Allahu Akbar*
   Allah is greater, Allah is greater
2. *ash-hadu an la ilaha illa'llah*
   I witness that there is no god but Allah
3. *ash-hadu anna Muhammada'r-rasulullah*
   I witness that Muhammad is the Messenger of Allah
4. *hayya 'ala's-salah*
   Come to the prayer
5. *hayya 'ala'l-falah*
   Come to success
6. *qad qamati's-salah*
   The time for prayer has come
7. *Allahu Akbar, Allahu Akbar*
   Allah is greater, Allah is greater
8. *la ilaha illa'llah*
   There is no god but Allah

Awqat – Times of the Prayers

Name/ Time	Fard/ Obligatory	Sunna/ Recommended
Subh/ Dawn	2 rak'ats (Qur'an out loud)	2 rak'ats before[1]
Dhuhr/ Midday	4 rak'ats (Qur'an silent)	2+2 rak'ats before
		2 rak'ats after
'Asr/ After- noon	4 rak'ats (Qur'an silent)	2+2 rak'ats before
Maghrib/ Sunset	3 rak'ats (Qur'an out loud)	2 rak'ats after
'Isha'/ Night	4 rak'ats (Qur'an out loud)	2+1 rak'ats after[1]

---

1   The Sunna rak'ats before the prayer of Subh are called Fajr, and those after the prayer of 'Isha' are

It is, of course, permitted and praiseworthy to do rak'ats at other times, particularly in the morning after sunrise and during the last part of the night, but these are entirely voluntary. No rak'ats should be done between the prayer of Subh and sunrise or between the prayer of 'Asr and Maghrib.

---

called Shafa' and Witr. They should never be missed.

The Performance of One Rak'at

Face towards qibla – the direction of Makka.
Make the intention to do the particular prayer
you are about to perform for Allah alone.
Raise your hands level with your shoulders
and lower them to your side, saying Allahu
Akbar, audibly – Allah is greater.
This is called the Takbir al-Ihram and with
the saying of it, you enter the state of prayer.

1. QIYAM – STANDING

Stand upright with your feet slightly apart,
your head straight, and your eyes lowered.
Surat al-Fatiha (in every rak'at)
[Note: In the Maliki school, *"Bismillahi'r-
Rahmani'r-Rahim"* is not recited in the Fatiha
in the prayer.]
Other recitation of Qur'an (first 2 rak'ats),
preferably at least 3 ayats long. Then: *Allahu
Akbar* – Allah is greater.

2. RUKU' – BOWING

Bow with your back parallel to the ground,
your legs straight, your hands gripping your
knees.

Subhana rabbiya'l-'adhim – Glory to my Lord, the Immense. (3 times)

Then while rising, the Imam recites in congregational prayer, or you do if you are praying alone:

sami'a llahu liman hamidah – Allah hears the one who praises Him.

Then the mu'adhdhin who called the prayer replies, or you do yourself if you are praying alone:

Allahumma Rabbana wa laka'l-hamd – O Allah, our Lord, praise is Yours.

3. QIYAM – STANDING

As before. *Allahu Akbar* – Allah is greater.

4. SAJDA – PROSTRATION

You touch the ground with your forehead, the tip of your nose, your palms, your knees, and the tips of your toes facing forwards.

subhana'l-rabbiya'l-a'la – Glory to my Lord, the High (3 times).

Then while sitting back:

Allahu Akbar – Allah is greater.

5. Julus – Sitting

You sit on your left foot turned under.
Your right foot remains upright against your right thigh. Your hands rest on your knees.
Allahumma'ghfirli wa'rhamni – O Allah, forgive me and give me mercy.
Then while going into sajda again:
Allahu Akbar – Allah is greater.

6. Sajda – Prostration

As before: *subhana'l-rabbiya'l-a'la* – Glory to my Lord, the High (3 times).
Then while rising:
Allahu Akbar – Allah is greater.

7. Qiyam – Standing

After the first and third rak'ats except after Maghrib.
Surat al-Fatiha (in every rak'at)
Other recitation of Qur'an (first and second rak'at only) at least 3 ayats long.

8. Julus – Sitting

After second and last rak'ats. The Tashahhud in second and final rak'at.

Salat 'ala'n-Nabi in final rak'at only.
Finally turning your head to the right say:
As-salamu 'alaykum – Peace be upon you.

2. Salat – The Prayer

Surat al-Fatiha – The Opening

(This Sura must be recited in every rak'at)
1. *Bismillahi'r-Rahmani'r-Rahim*

   In the Name of Allah, the Universally Merciful, the Specifically Merciful,
2. *al-hamdu lillahi rabbi'l-'alamin*

   All praise to Allah, the Lord of all the worlds,
3. *ar-rahmani'r-rahim*

   The Universally Merciful, the Specifically Merciful,
4. *maliki yawmi'd-din*

   the King of the Day of the Accounting.
5. *iyyaka na'budu wa iyyaka nasta'in*

   You alone we worship, You alone we ask for help.
6. *ihdina's-sirata'l-mustaqim*

   Guide us on the Straight Path,
7. *sirata'l-ladhina an'amta 'alayhim*

   The Path of those You have blessed,

   ghayri'l-maghdubi 'alayhim wala'd-dallin

   Not of those with anger upon them nor those who are astray.

   Amin.

Surat al-Ikhlas – Pure Sincerity

1. *Bismillahi'r-Rahmani'r-Rahim*
In the Name of Allah, the Universally Merciful, the Specifically Merciful,
2. *qul huwa' llahu ahad*
Say: He is Allah, One,
3. *Allahu's-samad*
Allah, the Endless Sustainer of All.
4. *lam yalid wa lam yulad*
He does not give birth, and is not born.
5. *wa lam yakul lahu kufu'an ahad*
No one is equal to Him.

Surat an-Nas – People

1. *Bismillahi'r-Rahmani'r-Rahim*
   In the Name of Allah, the Universally Merciful, the Specifically Merciful,
2. *Qul a'udhu bi rabbi'n-nas*
   Say: I seek refuge with the Lord of people,
   maliki'n-nas ilahi'n-nas
   the King of people, the God of people,
3. *min sharri'l-waswasi'l-khannas*
   From the evil of the deceitful whisperer,
4. *alladhi yuwaswisu fi suduri'n-nas*
   Who whispers in the breasts of people,
5. *mina'l-jinnati wa'n-nas*
   of Jinn and people.

At-Tashahhud – Witnessing

(Said in the sitting position of the prayer)
At-tahiyyatu lillah az-zakiyatu lillah
at-tayyibatu's-salawatu lillah
Greetings are for Allah and purity is for Allah,
the best prayers are for Allah.
As-salamu 'alayka ayyuha'n-nabiyyu
wa rahmatu'llahi wa barakatuhu
Peace be upon you, O Prophet and the mercy
of Allah and His blessing.
As-salamu 'alayna wa 'ala 'ibadi-llahi's-salihin
Peace be upon us and on the right-acting
worshippers of Allah.
Ash-hadu an la ilaha illa'llahu wahdahu
la sharika lah
I witness that there is no god but Allah alone,
with no partner.
wa ash-hadu anna Muhammadan 'abduhu wa
rasuluh
And I witness that Muhammad is His slave
and Messenger.

In the final Julus add this prayer on the Prophet:
*Allahumma salli 'ala Muhammadin wa 'ala ali
Muhammad*
O Allah, bless Muhammad and the family of
Muhammad
kama sallayta 'ala Ibrahima wa 'ala ali Ibrahim
as you blessed Ibrahim and the family of
Ibrahim,
wa barik 'ala Muhammadin wa 'ala ali Muhammad
and pour baraka on Muhammad and on the
family of Muhammad
kama barakta 'ala Ibrahima wa 'ala ali Ibrahim
as you poured baraka on Ibrahim and the
family of Ibrahim
fi'l-'alamin innaka hamidun majid
In all the worlds. You are Praiseworthy,
Glorious.

Allah says in the Qur'an:
'Prayer keeps you from profanity and bad actions.'

Muhammad, peace and blessings of Allah be
upon him, said:
'Tell me, if one of you had a stream running
at his door and he bathed in it five times every
day, would any dirt be left on him?'

He was answered, 'No, no dirt would be left.'
He continued, 'It is the same with the five
prayers. By them Allah wipes out every wrong
action.'

3. ZAKAT

1. Property subject to Zakat

1. **Livestock**
   Camels; cattle; sheep and goats [Not horses, mules, donkeys]
   Nisab. Camels 5; cattle, 30, sheep 40
2. **Crops**
   Grains, oil seeds, dates, raisins (not fruits, spices, green vegetables)
   Nisab: 5 wasqs (300 sa's)
   10th if naturally irrigated, 20th if irrigated.
   Due when the crop is ripe
3. **Cash**
   200 silver dirhams or 20 gold dinars
   2 $\frac{1}{2}$% is due.
4. **Trading goods**
   Turnover, stock

PRECONDITIONS:

1. They are goods not subject to zakat in themselves.
2. They were purchased.
3. They were acquired with the purpose of trade.
4. The price of the goods is money or goods. acquired by purchase.

5. The goods are sold for cash
6. A year has passed since they were acquired or zakat paid on them

3. Zakat – The Poor Tax

2. Preconditions for owing zakat

1. Being Muslim
2. Being free (guardian pays for children or insane)
3. Owning the nisab (minimum amount)
4. Having it for a year (for cash and livestock)
5. Arrival of the collector (for livestock)
6. Lack of debt in money

3. Preconditions for its validity

1. The intention to pay zakat.
2. Immediate distribution of zakat (it should be paid close to the place where it became obligatory)
3. Paying it after it is obligatory
4. Paying it to a just imam if he exists or to the eight categories entitled to receive it

4. Preconditions for the person receiving it

1. Being free (except for categories 4 and 5 on p.30)
2. Being a Muslim
3. Not being from the Banu Hashim

5. Preconditions for the zakat collector

1. They are just and fair
2. They are knowledgeable.

6. Those entitled to receive zakat (8 categories)

1. Someone who does not possess enough food for a year.
2. Someone who does not own anything;
3. Zakat agents
4. Reconciling hearts to bring them to Islam or to new Muslims to make their faith firm
5. Freeing believing slaves;
6. Paying the debts of debtors.
7. Mujahids, murabits and spies.
8. Travellers wh o lack the funds to return home.

4. SIYAM – FASTING

Fasting is obligatory for every adult Muslim
in Ramadan who is physically able to fast

Exceptions (Excuses)

Excuses for not fasting are:

1. Those who are ill (fasting will make them worse or delay recovery)
2. Those who are very old and too weak to fast
3. Menstruating women or women with post-partum bleeding
4. Those who are travelling
5. Those who are insane
6. Nursing women if their health or the health of their child is in danger
7. Pregnant women if their health or the health of their child is in danger

Starting and Ending the Fast

Starts by sighting the moon or 30 days of Shawwal.

You must make the intention to fast before dawn.

You can make the intention for the entire month if the fast is continuous.

Break the fast as soon as possible and delay sahur (pre-dawn meal).

A supplication to be said after breaking the fast is:

Allahumma laka sumtu wa bika aamantu wa ʿala rizqika aftartu, faʾghfir li maa qadamtu wa maa akhkhartu, ya rabbaʾl-ʿaalameen

O Allah, for You I have fasted and in You I believe and on Your provision I have broken my fast, so forgive me what I have sent on ahead and what I have left behind, O Lord of all the worlds.

The fast ends by sighting the moon or 30 days of Ramadan.

Things which invalidate the fast

Eating or drinking
Sexual intercourse
Emission of sperm
Smoking
Making oneself vomit deliberately
Menstruation or post natal bleeding

Making up Missed Days

Days missed must be made up before the next Ramadan.

If not made up before Ramadan, fidya is owed.

Breaking the fast deliberately without excuse entails kaffara.[2]

---

2   Kaffara: feeding sixty poor people with a mudd, or fasting two continuous months or freeing a slave

Fidya

Fidya is feeding a poor Muslim with a mudd of the predominant food of the land.

Someone who fails to make up missed days before the next Ramadan owes fidya.

Old people and the chronically ill who cannot fast owe fidya for missed days. In the case of the elderly, it is only recommended in the Maliki school.

A nursing woman who does not fast out of fear for her child owes fidya.

A mudd is about half a kilo.

Zakat al-Fitr

Zakat al-fitr is an obligation at the end of Ramadan.

1. A father pays for his children (except adult males).
2. A husband pays for his wife.
3. It is a sa' of food (about 2 kilos).
4. It is paid in food (usually grains, like rice).
5. It should be paid before the 'Eid prayer.
6. It is given to poor Muslims.
7. If unpaid before the prayer, it is still owed until it is paid.

Fasting Du'as

What is said before one breaks the fast:

Allahumma laka sumtu wa bika aamantu [wa 'alayka tawakkaltu] wa 'ala rizq-ika aftartu

(O Allah! I fasted for You and I believe in You [and I put my trust in You] and I break my fast with Your sustenance)

What one says after having broken the fast

dhahaba'dh-dhama'u wab'tallatil-'uruuqu, wa thabata'l-arju insha'Allah

The thirst has vanished, the veins have been wetted and the reward is established – Insha-Allah.

Allah says in the Qur'an:

'*O you who believe, fasting is prescribed for you as it was prescribed for those before you so that hopefully you will be godfearing.*'

Muhammad, peace and blessings of Allah be upon him, said:

"Anyone who fasts experiences two joys. He is joyful when he breaks his fast, and he will joyful because of his fasting when he meets his Lord."

5. HAJJ – PILGRIMAGE

Hajj is the pilgrimage to Makka

Preconditions

1. Being an adult
2. Being sane
3. Being able to perform it
4. Being a Muslim
4. Being able to perform it
4. Does not entail excessive hardship
5. There is security of life and property
6. For women, a mahram (male relative) or safe   companions

Pillars

Ihram
Sa'y
Tawaf al-Ifada
Standing at 'Arafat

5. Hajj – The Pilgrimage To Makka

Ihram

1. Intention
2. Miqat: place before which one must go into ihram
3. Forbidden things:
   Oiling the hair or body
   Removing nails
   Removing hair
   Removing dirt
   Using scent
   Covering the face (and head for men)
   Wearing stitched clothing for men
   If you do any of the above, you owe fidya.
4. Saying the Talbiya[3] which is stopped in tawaf and sa'y and after reaching 'Arafa.
5. It is Sunna to take a ghusl and pray two rak'ats before ihram.

---

3 Talbiya: *"Labbayk Allahumma, labbayk. Labbayk, la sharika lak. labbayk. Inna'l-hamda wa'n-ni'mata laka wa'l-mulk. La sharika lak"* (At Your service, O Allah, at Your service. At Your service, You have no partner. At Your service. Praise and blessing are Yours and the kingdom. You have no partner.)

Sa'y

1. Seven circuits
2. Start at Safwa and end at Marwa
3. Preceded by wudu'
4. Being in purity
5. Going fast between the green markers

Tawaf al-Ifada

1. Must be in wudu'
2. Private parts must be covered
3. Having the House to one's left
4. Being outside the Shadharwan and Hijr
5. It has seven circuits, starting and ending at the Black Stone
6. Must be done inside the mosque
7. Greeting the Stone when passed in each circuit
8. Trotting in the first three circuits
9. Two rak'ats after tawaf at the Maqam Ibrahim
10. Drinking Zamzam water
11. Tawaf al-Ifada is done from after dawn on the Day of Sacrifice

Standing at 'Arafat

1. Shortening the prayers and combining them
2. Supplication
3. Standing at 'Arafa for a time on 9th Dhu'l-Hijja
4. Leave 'Arafa for Muzdalifa after Maghrib
5. Maghrib and 'Isha' done at Muzdalifa

Types of Hajj

1. Ifrad: hajj on its own
2. Tamattu': performing 'umra in the months in which one does hajj
3. Qiran: Intending to perform both 'umra and hajj

Description of Hajj

1. Ihram
2. Talbiyya
3. Qiran: Intending to perform both 'umra and hajj
4. Sa'y
5. Going to Mina on 8th Dhu'l-Hijja
6. Going to 'Arafa after sunrise
7. Night at Muzdalifa, gathering pebbles (49 or 70)
8. Stoning Jamrat al-'Aqaba
9. Slaughtering and shaving the head
10. Tawaf al-ifada
11. Leave ihram
12. Return to Mina
13. Stoning 3 Jamrat for 2 or 3 days
14. Farewell Tawaf

Lightning Source UK Ltd.
Milton Keynes UK
UKHW011005170919
349935UK00007B/120/P